DR. D. K. OLUKOYA

ABRAHAM'S CHILDREN in BONDAGE

ABRAHAM'S CHILDREN IN BONDAGE

DR. D. K. OLUKOYA

ABRAHAM'S CHILDREN IN BONDAGE
© 2010 DR. D. K. OLUKOYA
ISBN 978-978-49174-13-0
June 2010

Published by:
Mountain of Fire and Miracles Ministries Press
13, Olasimbo Street, Onike, Yaba, Lagos.

All Scripture quotation is from the King James Version of the Bible

All rights reserved.
We prohibit reproduction in whole or part without written permission

CONTENTS

DEALING WITH SPIRITUAL BONDAGE 5
CHILDREN IN BONDAGE 6
THE CHILDREN OF ABRAHAM 8
HINDRANCES 10
MOVING BY FAITH 11

WHY ABRAHAM'S CHILDREN ARE IN TRAVAIL 13
SATANIC VICTIMS 14

FAITH FOR POSSESSING ABRAHAM'S BLESSINGS 21

OVERPOWERING SATANIC WEAPONS 27
A WOLF IN SHEEP'S CLOTHING 29
BACK TO SENDER 30
WHAT DOES FALL DOWN AND DIE MEAN? 31
WHO CARRIES SATANIC ARROWS ABOUT? 31

REARRANGING THE PROBLEM 33
ONE SECURES VICTORY AGAINST 450 35

WHEN THE ENEMY REARRANGES PROBLEMS 39
VIGILANCE IS KEY 40
TOO HOT TO HANDLE 42

OTHER BOOKS BY DR. D. K. OLUKOYA 44

CHAPTER ONE

DEALING WITH SPIRITUAL BONDAGE

"And behold there was a woman which hath a spirit of infirmity eighteen years, and was bowed together; and could in no wise lift up herself." **Luke 13:11**

It is possible that a sickness could be engineered by an evil spirit. In such a case doctors are virtually helpless. Their knowledge can only deal with the physical and not the spiritual. Applying a physical solution to a spiritual sickness will only worsen the situation as the physical medication will only act as a fertilizer to strengthen the problem. This may also result in the victim acquiring a new demon that may make him become a drug addict.

CHILDREN IN BONDAGE

If you have any infirmity in your body, you have a wonderful opportunity to deal with it because God did not design infirmity for His children. He knows that they will not be able to serve Him with infirmity. Although having the spirit of infirmity will not disqualify one from getting to heaven, but it will ravage one's body here on earth. You cannot do much for the Lord with a sick body. Infirmity may be ravaging your body while your spirit can make it to heaven. Therefore pray a prayer of command like this:
Every infirmity in my life, dry up from the roots, in the name of Jesus
Doctors certainly have terminologies for all sicknesses, including the spiritual ones.

"And when Jesus saw her, he called her to him, and said unto her, woman thou art loosed from thine infirmity." **Luke 13:12**
Jesus could see the rope with which she was bound hence he loosed her from it.

> *"And he laid his hands on her: and immediately she was made straight, and glorified God. And the ruler of the synagogue answered with indignation, because that Jesus had healed on the sabbath day, and said unto the people, There are six days in which men ought to work: in them therefore come and be healed, and not on the sabbath day. The Lord then answered him, and said, Thou hypocrite, doth not each one of you on the sabbath loose his ox or his ass from the stall, and lead him away to watering? And ought not this woman, being a daughter of Abraham, whom satan hath bound, lo, these eighteen years, be loosed from this bond on the sabbath day?"* Luke 13:13-16

Her adversaries were not bothered about her plight but were more concerned about the breaking of their law. They wanted people healed only from Monday to Friday but not on the Sabbath day. These were enemies right inside the church! I pray that those who are not happy with your progress shall be disgraced, in Jesus' name. Beloved, the interesting thing here is that though that woman was a daughter of Abraham, she was tied with an invisible rope. By great faith in God, her spiritual father, Abraham, was made a source of blessings to the whole world and she, like many today, must have appropriated the blessings to herself. In spite of this she was still in bondage.

Abraham did not have access to the reference and study Bibles as we have today. He had neither the computer Bible nor any example to follow, yet he exercised a high level of faith that even challenged God to make him a source of blessing to the whole world. This is why people all over the world tend to appropriate the blessings of Abraham to themselves.

THE CHILDREN OF ABRAHAM

Who are the children of Abraham?

> *"Even as Abraham believed God, and it was accounted to him for righteousness. Know ye therefore that they which are of faith, the same are the children of Abraham. And the scripture, foreseeing that God would justify the heathen through faith, preached before the gospel unto Abraham, saying, In thee shall all nations be blessed. So then they which be of faith are blessed with faithful Abraham. For as many as are of the works of the law are under the curse: for it is written, Cursed is every one that continueth not in all things which are written in the book of the law to do them. But that no man is justified by the law in the sight of God, it is evident: for, the just shall live by faith. And the law is not of faith: but, the man that doeth them shall live in them. Christ hath redeemed us from the curse of the law, being made a curse for us: for it is written, Cursed is every one that hangeth on a tree: That the blessing of Abraham might come on the Gentiles through Jesus Christ; that we might receive the promise of the Spirit through faith. Brethren, I speak after the manner of men; Though it be but a man's covenant, yet if it be confirmed, no man disannulleth, or addeth thereto. Now to Abraham and his seed were the promises made. He saith not, And to seeds, as of many; but as of one, And to thy seed, which is Christ."* **Galatians 3:6-16**

> *"And if ye be Christ's, then are ye Abraham's seed, and heirs according to the promise."* **Galatians 3:29**

Those who are in the household of faith, who belong to Christ, are the children of Abraham. Therefore if you do not have the faith of Abraham you cannot claim to belong to Abraham. And if you are Abraham's seed, you will behave like him. God intends all believers to become Abraham's seeds and to inherit his blessings. The woman in our text belonged to Abraham but she was in bondage. The same thing is true of most believers today.

Many Abraham's children are bound. Their situation could be likened to the story of a gorilla that was put in a cage for years. The enemies of the beast visited it and threw stones at it. Its friends came as well to give it banana. It kept on living like this for a long time until a white man came forward to buy it. His offer was accepted and he brought it out of the cage and kept it in a good environment to enjoy liberty. But to the amazement of the white man, the gorilla could not appropriate its freedom because it was used to confinement in the cage. A lot of people are like this.

A person under bondage cannot enjoy the blessings of Abraham. The Bible tells us that the blessings of Abraham extend to both our physical and material prosperities. If the spirit is sick, the sickness would affect the physical and this explains why the devil is first interested in ravaging the inside of a man. Knowing fully that when the inside is polluted, every other thing you set your hands on will equally be affected. The spiritual, physical and material matters are the three common areas in which a person can be under bondage.

HINDRANCES

A person can be under the bondage of drug or debt: bondage is bondage. There is no small bondage. But when you operate in the faith of Abraham, people may tend to view you as being fanatical, they may feel you are intolerant of others. But when you begin to reap the blessings, they will begin to wonder how it happened.

> A man once told the story of a colleague at his place of work who was a prayer addict. He said he always used his free period to pray while others were either at the canteen or doing something else. Then things started to happen: he was soon made a supervisor. Later on, he became a manager. Eventually, he resigned his appointment only to come with a big car to visit his former colleagues. He was still praying all the while. But people often describe those who pray like this as mad. Those who operate in faith are called mad people because faith is not logic. Whoever comes to God with the expectation to receive from Him must first of all forget whatever knowledge he has. What faith attempts to do may sometimes be illogical, unreasonable and unscientific.

While I was studying abroad, we used to have students' Christian movement which met every Friday for fellowship. We used to invite men of God to come and preach to us. One day, a man was invited, though a white man, his complexion showed he had been terribly affected by the scorching sun. When he started to minister he said: "Do you know that there is a particular witch that goes about every church in this city to rain curses." The white man sitting by my side exclaimed: "This is outrageous!" But I admitted within me that the man got the point, even though that was the first time I heard a white man mention the subject of witchcraft. He then asked us to pray a corporate prayer, which we were not used to praying.

As the prayer began, confusion ensued. The lady that led the praise worship was the first person that was carried out. We could see that the man carried the touch of power. This man told us what happened in a rural area of India which was a very long distance to a hospital. A snake bit one man and in the midst of the perplexing situation, a man surfaced from nowhere and issued a command that the snake's poison should come out, in the name of the Lord. Instantly, the poison started to flow out. The man said even though he had been a Christian for long, he was greatly challenged by the faith of the Christian Indian.

MOVING BY FAITH

Abraham was asked by God to sacrifice Isaac, his son, who was his dearest treasure and future hope. He did not argue with God for he knew that it was God who provided the son and could provide another Isaac by resurrection. It was the same Abraham who argued with God when He wanted to destroy Sodom and Gomorrah. He did not even tell Sarah or Isaac himself or his slaves about his adventure with God. This would have been termed sheer madness by his people.

There is no such thing as bad news for a person moving in faith. Bad news poses a challenge to our faith and as we move forward in faith, we have the courage to challenge God with bigger problems that come our way. Many people pray against cancer but have not succeeded in dealing with common headache. Many people are praying that God should remove every obstacle on their way, but they forget that that would make them lazy and good for nothing soldiers to God.

When I was in the junior school, I was always beaten up by the grown-ups. As I kept complaining, somebody encouraged me to try to fight back whenever they came to attack me. One day, one grown-up challenged me and I dipped my fingers into his eyes so that he could not see. Then I carried him and threw him on the ground and took to my heels. From that day he kept a distance from me. What did I do to deliver myself? I flexed my muscle and it worked. This underscores the saying that the best method of defence is to attack. God has not called His children to be harassed by the enemy.

PRAYER POINTS

1. Every dark power assigned to follow my life, turn back and attack your senders, in the name of Jesus.

2. Every door opened to spiritual bondage in my life, be closed by the blood of Jesus.

3. Every spiritual bondage in my life, break, in the name of Jesus.

4. Doors of affliction in my life, be closed for ever, in the name of Jesus.

5. Every dark power visiting me in the night, your time is up, die, in the name of Jesus.

CHAPTER TWO

WHY ABRAHAM'S CHILDREN ARE IN TRAVAIL

The question now is why are the children of Abraham always in trouble? What are the reasons behind the travails of Abraham's children?

1. Sin:

Abraham's children are wedded to sin, and since Mr. Sin is the husband whilst the sinner is the wife, an evil covenant is formed. Mr. Sin will continue to force the sinner to commit sin regularly. As long as the wedding is in place, trouble will continue to have a field day in the sinner's life.

SATANIC VICTIMS

Sometime ago, I went to preach somewhere and a boy of 16 was brought to me for prayers. His problem was that he was addicted to prostitutes. He had stolen about forty thousand naira from his mother to patronize prostitutes. He told me he was in a senior secondary school and that he was born again. Here was a born again Christian whose life had been damaged by the sin of immorality. He was so devastated that all his private parts were full of terrible sores. Nevertheless, he maintained he could not stop going to prostitutes. This is an example of a life married to sin.

At times, when you give some people prayer points and tell them to keep away from anger if they want answers to the prayers, they will say they cannot guarantee that. It is because there is an evil marriage in place. If you remove the issue of sin from the Bible, there will be no Bible, and there would not have been the need for the Saviour to come to the world to sacrifice Himself for mankind.

You may attend a lot of Bible colleges, but if sin is not dealt with in your life, all the knowledge you might have required amount to nothing. All your lecture topics would be mere theories. That is why the Bible says that people will shun sound teachings in the last days and would heap up for themselves teachers with itching ears.

2. Ignorance:

The second reason Abraham's children are in trouble is ignorance.

"My people are destroyed for lack of knowledge."
Hosea 4:6

This is not referring to satanic people, but God's own people. If Samson had known that the lap of Delilah would spell doom for him, he would have fled. A person can be so stupid in ignorance that God may find it difficult to help him.

> I told a sister 13 years ago that she needed to go for deliverance ministration. She told me she did not believe in deliverance because her church was not preaching it. She said once you believed and you were born again, you were automatically delivered. To my surprise, she came calling after 13 years that she needed deliverance. For those 13 years, she was suffering because of ignorance.

Another lady was staying with her husband in England. One day, she had a dream that a white lady came to strip her of her wedding gown and ring. When she related the story to her husband during breakfast the following morning, he dismissed it as a figment of her imagination and as such nothing was done about it. But before the week ran out, a white woman had already taken over her home while she found herself back in Nigeria! Why? Ignorance.

If immediately she woke up from that dream, she prayed to reverse the dream, what happened to her would have been averted. Even though she was born again, she did not know how to deal with the dream, hence there was nothing the Almighty could do in that situation. Even the Bible says that some people are bent on exhibiting wilful ignorance. I pray that God would have mercy on such people.

3. **Breaking the laws of faith:**

This can also lead Abraham's children into bondage. When you break the laws of faith, the promise of Abraham would not be fulfilled in your life. What does it mean to break the laws of faith?

i. **Faith must be rooted in the word of God and not in your brain or what you think or feel or your personal opinion.**

ii. **Faith must be confessed with the mouth.** The Bible says, "If any of you shall say unto the mountain, be thou removed and be cast into the sea and do not doubt in his heart, but believe that what he had said shall come to pass, it shall be so." In the beginning, before things began to happen, the Bible says, "God said, Let there be light." God spoke and things began to happen.

iii. **Faith must be blind to opposing circumstances.** That is, your circumstances may look hostile and unfavourable, but you should be blind to it.

iv. **Faith must not be moved by sight.** The Bible says, "We walk by faith and not by sight." Once you allow what you are seeing to move you, faith jumps out of the window of your life.

v. **Faith must continuously give praises to God.** When a person is always full of praises and thanks to God, his faith will be on top. Do not say, "Why should I praise Him when He has not done anything for me." A pastor once talked of a believer who was always grateful unto God by giving sacrificially unto God. This believer was operating a salt business. One day, a great flood flushed his large stock of salt away. When his pastor heard of this unfortunate incident, he was afraid to visit him because he could hardly find words of the Bible to console and encourage him. But as he summed up courage to visit him, he found to his amazement, the man and members of his family rejoicing. He said, "Pastor, don't worry. God took away my stock of salt to make room for a larger one." So, when the devil sees that people are always happy and rejoicing in a particular family, he runs away. But if he finds otherwise, he would pitch his tent with them.

vi. **Faith does not make negative confessions.** Someone who moves by faith will not be confessing evil to himself. He will not say, "Oh, this headache, or this asthma will kill me." No. You must speak good things to your life and believe that all the problems are gone with Christ on the cross. One way most of us pull down this country is through our confessions.

One day I was in a bank and I heard a woman saying, "Oh, this country is finished," simply because the bank official complained of her signature being irregular. She forgot that we are still living in this country, whether we like it or not, and if it is good, we will enjoy it and if it is bad, it is to our disadvantage. Why do we have to destroy the country with our mouths? Uttering words like 'bastard,' 'that your foolish dad will soon come,' 'dunce,' 'idiot,' etc, to your children, will make them behave exactly like that.

vii. **Faith does not entertain wrong thoughts.** Some people contemplate suicide as a means of escaping the troubles of this world. A brother told me of a Christian who committed suicide in Zimbabwe and people began to wonder how a Christian could take his own life. But Zimbabwe is one of the enclaves of white men whose peculiarity is to commit suicide. So they told the Nigerian brother that the victim had gone to heaven to enjoy the peace he could not find on earth. A person who prays fervently for an accident-free journey and then begins to think negatively of the journey, is not operating in faith.

viii. **Faith must be back up by patience**

> *"That ye be not slothful but followers of them who through faith and patience inherit the promise."*
> **Hebrews 6:12**

According to this passage, faith must be married to patience. One of the greatest virtues that God gives to man is patience. Many people want to run faster than their legs can carry them. Some want to run 100 meters while they are still crawling. You need to be patient to allow God to sort out your life. You may say your application is being delayed. Well, it may be that God wants to remove somebody for you in that company or He may first of all want to close the mouth of the lions that are sent there by the enemy to attack you. When you plant maize, you don't dig it up every morning to check how it is growing. If you do that, the maize will not grow. You need to exercise patience with it.

ix. **Faith does not give up.** If you are a child of Abraham, you will not give up. I have witnessed many impossible situations in my life, which the God of Abraham, Isaac and Jacob had turned around. This is the God that Elijah called upon on Mount Carmel and He answered by fire.

x. **Faith must be resistant to discouragement and fear.** That is why you must not have fearful and discouraging friends; otherwise you have work to do. If your faith is subject to discouragement and fear, it is not the Abraham-type of faith but the faith of Thomas. Thomas said, "Except I move close to him, see the hole of the nails in his hands and thrust my finger through them, I will not believe." And it was a shameful thing for him when he saw Jesus, for Jesus declared to him that blessed were those who did not see and yet believed. The faith of Thomas is synonymous to that of modern-day doctors and scientists who believe in observation and experiment.

xi. **Faith must be released to operate.** Perhaps an illustration will serve to explain this: A woman in the Bible decided within herself from home not to be distracted by the crowd. She said, "If I can touch the helm of His garment, I shall be made whole." She released her faith and received her desired miracle without 'permission.' But Jesus knew what she did, because He was aware of the virtue that went out of Him.

xii. **Faith is fed by the word of God, but starved by the word of the devil.** The devil is the best preacher. Therefore if you listen to him, the faith in you will be starved. He will say, "There you are, those who are to minister to you have left before you got there, in spite of all your beauty, you are still waiting and praying to get married. For how long will you do that?" If you listen to him he will destroy you.

xiii. **Faith never cries, grumbles or complains.** You should not become a modern-day Jeremiah.

xiv. **Faith forgets past failures.** You don't say because your prayer has not been answered, you will give up your faith. No.

xv. **Faith is quenched by living in any known sin.**

PRAYER POINTS:

1. Every enemy of Abraham's blessings in my life, be bound, in Jesus' name.

2. Lord, magnetize angels of blessing to me, in the name of Jesus.

3. Every spirit working against me in my household, be exposed and be disgraced, in Jesus' name.

4. I cast out every spirit of infirmity, in the name of Jesus.

5. Every owner of infirmity, carry your load, in the name of Jesus.

6. Every longstanding infirmity, I destroy your feet by fire, in the name of Jesus.

7. I refuse to live with any sickness, in the name of Jesus.

CHAPTER THREE

FAITH FOR POSSESSING ABRAHAM'S BLESSINGS

1. Faith does not work for those who want to operate with other people's timetable:

    Your faith cannot work when you are comparing yourself with others, because what you are basing your faith on is not the plan of God for you. We have to be very careful about this. In Psalm 73, we see a man that wanted to make a comparison and found out that he was making a great mistake.

2. Faith is never envious of other people:

    If somebody is doing very well, you don't have to envy him. Rather you have to support him in prayers. The more you do that, the more God will bless you. The spirit of envy is from the pit of hell fire and it destroys very quickly. Also, when you take advice from envious people, you get into trouble. A sister had problems with her husband and went to a friend for counsel. The friend told her that she must not take nonsense from her husband. She advised: "If the man talks nonsense, you give it back to him raw." And the sister said, "If I do that, there will be quarrel." Her friend replied, "Ah! That is the only way you can deliver yourself from somebody that wants to be controlling you any how."

    Sadly, the person giving the counsel to this sister was practically a slave to her own husband. She would not say one word when her husband began to talk and here she was, counseling somebody else to be rebellious to her husband because she was envious of that woman. No sooner than the former take the advice of the latter than trouble started in her home. When she ran to this 'counselor' one night to tell her that she had been thrown out, she said, "I am sorry, I don't want my husband to meet you here, it will cause trouble. Take your things and go." The shocked sister shot back: "But you are the one that advised me." The evil counselor countered: "Anyone can advise anybody. Sometimes, it works and other times it does not. So, it is not my fault."

3. **Faith focuses on God alone:**

It does not start looking for alternatives but God alone. The moment Peter removed his eyes from Jesus, he began to sink; another law took over him, the law of doubt. So faith focuses on God alone and it does not look for alternatives. This is the blind Bartimeaus' kind of faith. He cried out, "Jesus, Son of David, have mercy on me," and he was not ready to stop until Jesus showed up.

4. **Faith rejoices in the Lord always:**

No matter what the situation is, faith rejoices in the Lord always. Sometimes what a person sees as a setback could be a divinely appointed staircase to climb into a higher realm. But if you look at it as a setback and get depressed, faith jumps out.

5. **Faith is buried by worry and anxiety:**

When you are worried and anxious it will seem as if you had never prayed. Worry and anxiety nullify prayers. A white man friend of mine would always say, "Why pray, when you can worry?" He used to say so because praying and worrying do not go together. If you worry don't bother to pray or, you drop the worry and pray.

6. **Faith knows no impossibility:**

   Somebody who moves by faith must not work by sight. If you must move by sight you will never praise God.

7. **Faith must start in the heart:**

   "But what saith it? The word is nigh thee, even in thy mouth, and in thy heart; that is, the word of faith, which we preach. That if thou shalt confess with thy mouth the Lord Jesus, and shalt believe in thine heart that God hath raised him from the dead, thou shalt be saved. For with the heart man believeth unto righteousness; and with the mouth confession is made unto salvation" Faith must start in the heart and not in the head." **Romans 10:8-10**

8. **Faith must be expressed by words and actions:**

Once you believe God; begin to confess that what you are asking from Him is so. Once you believe God, begin to act on it.

Once a person breaks the law of faith, even if he is a child of Abraham, he will suffer. So the first reason Abraham's children suffer is because of sin. There are many people who are bound by their past bad memories. A person who is 42 years old and has given his life to Jesus may still be haunted by what he did or what happened to him 21 years ago.

Whenever something bad happened to him he would trace it to that incident that happened 21 years ago. And the person keeps asking God for forgiveness for the same thing all the time even after God had forgiven him. If you are in this kind of situation you must decide to get out of it. You must not allow any bad past ignorant memories to ruin your present life. Some people who probably were the ones that first introduced their younger sisters to sex and now found out that, that younger sister is living a worldly life, have these memories tormenting them. Some did abortion a long time ago, and when they gave their lives to Christ they confessed and God has forgiven them. Yet they are still harassed by what we call the spirit of abortion because they have not forgiven themselves.

The spirit of abortion, which generally leads to frustration and backwardness will harass anybody that has ever done any form of abortion before. Until you go for deliverance, and clear yourself from that spirit, frustration will trail you like a police detective. Once you have done deliverance and cut it off, you have to put the past where it belongs.

Sometime ago, a man who came to see me told me that somebody who was a member of a Pentecostal church offended him and that is why he does not like Pentecostal churches and their members. I said, "Okay, where is the person?" He said he died fifteen years ago. "So what do you want us to do now? Do you want us to bring him up from the grave so that he can apologise to you?" He said no. He was being limited by past memories.

We have cases of fathers who have slept with their own daughters, men and women who were unfaithful to their partners and people who have experienced serious tragedies and the enemy makes these memories to linger on so that these people continue to live in bondage. If you live in the past, you miss out of the blessings of Abraham. Some people even try to remove imaginary demons out of themselves instead of jumping out from the past.

There are some people, who each time they remember certain things that had happened in the past, their spirits go down and they suddenly become sad even if they were rejoicing before. If you are like that, you cannot have Abraham's blessings. There are some people who are going about with a heavy burden of things they cannot share with others in their spirits. Although they refuse to share them, they still stubbornly hang them in their memories. They have to get out of that or Abraham's blessings would be difficult to get. Many of us need to forgive ourselves since God has forgiven us and claim our liberty.

I want you to lay your hand on your chest and pray like this:

PRAYER POINTS:

1. Every internal chain, chaining my faith, break, in the name of Jesus.

2. O God, arise and give me a mountain - moving faith, in the name of Jesus.

3. Every anchor of doubt in my life, break, in the name of Jesus.

CHAPTER FOUR

OVERPOWERING SATANIC WEAPONS

"Lord Jesus, walk back into my past and erase every destructive memory, in the name of Jesus."

One reason why Abraham's children suffer is that they permit the operation of satanic weapons in their lives. The devil has a lot of weapons in his armory which he uses against Christians day and night. These satanic weapons are:

1. **Continuous feeling of unworthiness.**

2. **Anxiety.**

3. **Fear, which leads to lack of confidence.**

    Many people have become like that servant in the Bible who because of fear of failure, fear of being compared to others and fear of taking risks buried his talent. He refused to do anything because he was under the bondage of fear.

4. **Doubt.**

5. **Anger.**

6. **Guilt.**

Many have allowed the weapons of the enemy to prosper in their lives. You need to identify these things and loose yourself from them. When some people come to God, they do not believe that their lot is improving. Some actually say that things are getting worse. All their dreams are negative because they lack faith and cannot see with their spiritual eyes.

We have a lot of wicked satanic agents surrounding us. The first problem is that, they themselves hate one another so they cannot love others. The law says, "Love your neighbour as yourself."

You have to love yourself before you can love others. So if you don't hate yourself, you will not submit your life to the enemy. Jesus is here today to set people free.

The Bible says we should be as wise as a serpent and gentle as a dove. It also says, "I send you forth as sheep among wolves." The Bible calls those we are living with wolves. Now, for a sheep to operate among wolves, certain things must enter the life of the sheep that will paralyze the wolves no matter how tough the wolves are.

A WOLF IN SHEEP'S CLOTHING

Let us consider the following activity of knowing a wolf: Two sisters who live in England heard about Mountain of Fire and Miracles Ministries and came. The first was 39 years old. Their problem was that no man had ever proposed marriage to them. I counseled them to go for deliverance and they asked, "What does that mean?" I explained, feeling sorry for them, because immediately I saw them I knew that their own father was in charge of their case. As they were about going out, I asked them where they were going. They said, "We bought some things for daddy and we want to go and give them to him." I told them to go but they should not let him embrace them. They asked why I said so and I told them that if they allowed him to embrace them, their marriage would be postponed again. They could not understand that, so I simply urged them to do as I had told them.

They went home and gave their daddy the present. Predictably, the man did not want to touch the present, he only wanted to embrace them and they said, "No, daddy, just take the present," and the man declared, "You have been to that church." They asked him: "How did you know that?" He answered, "Don't worry, you are small girls." They asked which church, and he described it. At that level, they started to shiver.

They were now genuinely afraid and ran back to me and narrated their experience. Beloved, how can a man enter a covenant with powers of darkness to renew his own prosperity at the expense of his daughters' goodness? We have such agents surrounding us. Therefore, it is the duty of Abraham's children, though they look like sheep, to strike at them like thunder.

BACK TO SENDER

Somebody once wrote me a letter from here and said, "Dr. Olukoya, thank you very much for what God is doing here and what He is doing in your life." He continued, "But I have a question The question is this: suppose somebody who is a believer, is being attacked by a witch and the believer came for deliverance and prayed fire prayers that every arrow of witchcraft in his life should go back to sender and the arrows went back to sender giving rise to problems and afflictions in the life of the witch. If the witch found out she was about to die, and quickly ran to Mountain of Fire and Miracles Ministries and submitted herself for deliverance while also prayerfully sending back the arrows to the sender, would the arrows go back to the believer that originally sent it? That was question number 1. Question 2: In all these back to sender issues, who carries the arrows? Is it angels or demons? He wanted to know the transport vessels that take arrows from one spot to the other. Question 3: Why do you people pray that every spirit working against your progress should fall down and die, can a spirit die?

Let's take it one after the other. When the person carrying the witchcraft spirit decides to repent, the arrow will not harm him and the evil spirit of the witchcraft, which can never repent leaves his body and enters another person who makes himself or herself available. When the person who repented of witchcraft, sends the arrows back, they will not go back to the believer but the arrows will gather themselves and go back to Mr. Devil who originally manufactured them. That is the original sender.

WHAT DOES FALL DOWN AND DIE MEAN?

We call death, separation from God. If somebody is eternally separated from God, he goes to the bottomless pit; the place where evil spirits don't want to go. So when you say fall down and die, what you are saying is this: go to the bottomless pit and be locked up there forever. That is the meaning.

WHO CARRIES SATANIC ARROWS ABOUT?

Nobody has to carry satanic arrows. They fly about by themselves. They don't need wings because they can move by themselves. Angels don't need to carry them. In fact, what angels sometimes do is deflect them from us. We are going to pray now, but if you are reading this message and you are not born again, you have not given your life to Jesus Christ, the first thing you have to do to enjoy God's blessings is to give your life to Jesus.

If you don't do that, you cannot be called Abraham's child, let alone enjoy the benefits of Abraham. So, if you are not born again though you have been going to church, make the following confession: Father, in the name of Jesus, I surrender my life to you. I confess my sins and forsake them. I say bye-bye to the devil. Lord Jesus, come into my life and be my Lord and Saviour. I enter the kingdom of heaven. Thank you heavenly Father, in Jesus' name. Amen.

Pray these prayer points with holy aggression and holy madness and with the spirit of somebody that means business.

PRAYER POINTS:

1. Every satanic inspiration targeted against me, be paralyzed, in the name of Jesus.

2. *(Place one hand on your head and the other one on your stomach very close to the belly button as you take the following prayer point. Please, if as you are praying this prayer point you begin to feel dizzy, sit down and continue with it. It is very important):* Every seed of sorrow planted in my life, fall down and die, in the name of Jesus.

3. *Please, still retain your hand on your head and the other one on your belly button:* Any power that does not want to see me around, fall down and die, in the name of Jesus.

4. Every evil sun and evil moon, be disgraced, in the name of Jesus.

5. Begin to thank God for what He has done.

CHAPTER FIVE

REARRANGING THE PROBLEM

"Then Jerubbaal, who is Gideon, and all the people that were with him, rose up early, and pitched beside the well of Harod: so that the host of the Midianites were on the north side of them, by the hill of Moreh, in the valley. And the Lord said unto Gideon, The people that are with thee are too many for me to give the Midianites into their hands, lest Israel vaunt themselves against me, saying, Mine own hand hath saved me. Now therefore go to, proclaim in the ears of the people, saying, Whosoever is fearful and afraid, let him return and depart early from mount Gilead. And there returned of the people twenty and two thousand; and there remained ten thousand. And the Lord said unto Gideon, The people are yet too many; bring them down unto the water, and I will try them for thee there: and it shall be, that of whom I say unto thee, This shall go with thee, the same shall go with thee

; and of whomsoever I say unto thee, This shall not go with thee, the same shall not go. So he brought down the people unto the water: and the Lord said unto Gideon, Every one that lappeth of the water with his tongue, as a dog lappeth, him shalt thou set by himself; likewise every one that boweth down upon his knees to drink. And the number of them that lapped, putting their hand to their mouth, were three hundred men: but all the rest of the people bowed down upon their knees to drink water. And the Lord said unto Gideon, By the three hundred men that lapped will I save you, and deliver the Midianites into thine hand: and let all the other people go every man unto his place." **Judges 7: 17**

Israel had fallen into the sin of idolatry and this time as judgment, God permitted a horde of the Midianites to invade their land and rob them of their harvest. However, God raised Gideon to deliver them. The book of Judges is a book of problems, the kind of problems people encounter when they make God the tail and make themselves the head. Anytime you put God behind, there will always be problem. That was how the Israelites got into trouble.

The Lord commissioned Gideon to lead the Israelites in battle against the Midianites. In response to the Lord's command,

Gideon assembled an army by the well of Harod while the Midianites encamped somewhere in the north. Gideon had 32,000 men while the Midianites had 135,000. You can check the figures in Judges 8.

Gideon was facing 135,000 Midianites with 32,000 people, a ratio of about 4-1. Imagine Gideon's feeling when God told him that his men were too many. He asked those who were afraid to go home and 22,000 of them departed leaving him with 10,000 men to face the 135,000 Midianites yet, to the greater astonishment of Gideon God told him that the people were still too many. Then those who went down on both knees to drink water were eliminated and those who lapped as a dog were to go for the battle.

ONE SECURES VICTORY AGAINST 450

This takes us to the issue of lack of vigilance which is one essential characteristic in people that the enemy holds tight to enable him re-arrange problems in the lives of many.

> *"Be sober, be vigilant: because your adversary the devil, as a roaring lion, walketh about, seeking whom he may devour."* **I Peter 5:8**

Picture the soldiers who bowed on their knees to drink from the well; they could be attacked easily because they would have laid aside their weapons to be on both knees. They would not have seen the enemy approaching because they would have their faces buried inside the water, and the enemy would have overcome them. So, God removed them and left those who lapped like dogs.

When a dog drinks inside water it does not bury its nose inside the water, it just stretches out its tongue and laps. The men who lapped went down on one knee while retaining their weapons with one hand. So, they were vigilant. In their posture, they remained alert watching for any surprise attack by the enemy.

Only 300 of the 32,000 men passed the test and the ratio now became 450:1. They started with the ratio of 4-1 but by the time the Lord had dealt with them, the ratio fell to 450:1.

We have some lessons to learn from this. The Lord says "Be vigilant." The devil does not go on sabbatical. He never takes a holiday. When you think you need to relax and put your weapon down, the devil will release an unanticipated arrow.

The passage we read is very clear. The Almighty God looked at the 32,000 volunteers and said, "No, they are too many. Reduce the men. 22,000 went home and among the remaining 10,000 He selected only 300 and told Gideon that those were the men he should work with. What were the reasons for God's action?

1. **It is to prove that victory is from the Lord and not from man.**

    A man may boast and say all kinds of things. He may say that he is the best man in the world, yet victory is from the Lord and not from man. For example, nobody can scatter this country because of the prayer of the children of God. Anybody who wants to scatter it shall fall down and die.

    The Lord has a purpose for Nigeria in Africa and the world as far as the gospel is concerned. The Bible says that it is not by power or by might but by the Spirit of the living God. So, our personal foresight, planning ability, intelligence, technological know-how, etc cannot save us in the day of trouble. Victory is from the Lord.

2. **It is to prove that God does not work with a photocopy.**

    The fact that some men were not picked meant that they were not supposed to be there at all. Likewise many people just join the crowd of Christians without any conviction. God does not work on photocopy. He works on the original. Those rejected men were photocopies. They heard that there was going to be a battle and they joined, but they did not do so with conviction, so God had to discard them. Supposing you have to face persecution now for Jesus, can you be numbered among those who will stand firm?

3. **It was to prove that those eliminated men were not an asset to the cause. They were a liability.**

    They were not there wholeheartedly. They would have been a clog in the wheel of progress, so God had to remove them. I pray that every unprofitable friend, unprofitable crowd and unprofitable parasite in your life shall scatter, in the name of Jesus.

4. **It is to prove that God's strength does not depend on number.**

    So, stop saying that you are failing because nobody is supporting you. If God supports you, then every power in the universe is behind you. It is a very bad confession to say, "I have nobody to help me." We count people's heads but God counts the hearts. God is interested in the heart and not the head.

    A large percentage of these soldiers who bowed to drink the water took off their helmets, slackened their belts and removed their equipment, not minding the possibility of an ambush by the enemy. They forgot that they were at the warfront and that the enemy could come upon them anytime. They were drinking water as if all was well.

Only those who lapped without relaxing had the real soldier spirit. They were vigilant, never once taking their eyes off their leader. They were ready to spring to action anytime. God said, "These are the ones who can walk with me." Are you like that? Are you vigilant? Are you quick to detect sin in your life? Are you quick to notice when the Holy Spirit is saying, "Son, daughter, this is not the best for you?"

5. **It is to prove that many are called but few are chosen.**

    It is lack of vigilance that allows the enemy to be re-arranging problems in the lives of many people. Many Christians do not realize that they are fighting very terrible and clever spirits. Jeremiah 6:14 says, *"They have healed also the hurt of the daughter of my people slightly, saying, Peace, peace; when there is no peace."* They were patching things up when there was no peace. When you are not vigilant as a Christian, the enemy would re-arrange problems in your life.

Prayer points:

1. Every fetish material directed against my progress, be roasted, in Jesus' name.

2. Every meeting summoned against me by witchcraft powers, receive confusion, in the name of Jesus.

3. I shall laugh last, whether the enemy likes it or not, in Jesus' name.

4. Every power keeping me low, fall down and die, in the name of Jesus.

CHAPTER SIX

WHEN THE ENEMY REARRANGES PROBLEMS

What do we mean by re-arranging problems? In some parts of the world, suicide rate is now very high. People commit suicide so frequently and their governments do not seem to have an answer to the problem. Such governments spend money training experts to try to persuade those who want to kill themselves not to do so.

If somebody climbs a high building and is threatening to jump down, the trained people would be invited to the scene to persuade the person not to die. But most of the time, the people being persuaded would just jump and die. Suicide attempts got so rampant in a particular hotel in one city that anytime anybody came into the hotel lobby the first question the receptionist would ask is: "Are you staying or do you want to jump?"

In some places also, divorce rate is very high and sometimes a week after a wedding, the spouse files an action for divorce. Some couples start fighting at the altar. When the pastor says, "Read these after me," the bride would say to the bridegroom, "What kind of voice are you using to read? Why are you reading it with an unserious voice?" Some countries have come up with a regulation that a couple cannot divorce within three years of their marriage. This only amounts to re-arranging the problem.

VIGILANCE IS KEY

> The time we are living in now is a time of terrible spiritual conflicts. Although we have many Christian churches now, there are also many satanic churches around. Although we have an outpouring of the Holy Spirit, there are also intensive demonic activities. Although we have abundant life, there is also death around. We have a lot of prosperity and a lot of poverty too. We have a lot of love for God yet we have a lot of hatred for the Lord. Therefore, it is a time

for all Christians to be very vigilant and know that what most people sometimes describe as solution is not solution but a re-arrangement of the problem.

When you go to a herbalist, he will only re-arrange the problem. He would remove one problem and replace it with another clever one. When you go to a white garment prophet, he would trade your soul for temporary physical solution. When you go to an occultist, he would use your soul to form a covenant and give you temporary relief.

Sometime ago, a boy who had epilepsy was brought for prayers. Before then he had been taken somewhere and somebody did something diabolical which he was told to hang on his neck in the form of a cross. The boy thought that the problem was over only for it to get worse a few months later.

When he was brought to the church, the minister of God asked him to remove the cross from his neck and break it. He did so and found in it a paper on which was scribbled the phrase, "donated to satan." That boy thought he had been healed not knowing that all the so-called healer did for him was to re-arrange the problem.

Vigilance is very essential in these last days. The Bible says, "Be sober." That is, 'be quiet', 'be calculative,' 'have a sound mind,' 'be humble,' 'be attentive,' 'be careful.' The Bible does not stop there. It goes further to say, "Be vigilant." Why? Because the devil, your adversary, walketh about seeking whom he may devour.

TOO HOT TO HANDLE

Somebody shared the testimony of a sister with me. The sister was preaching the gospel in a street and a certain man invited her to share the gospel with him. She entered the man's house not knowing what the man had in mind. Suddenly, instead of the man to sit on the chair and listen to her, he slapped her on the chest and started chanting incantations. But everything he chanted to happen to the sister happened to him. He fell down and began to scream and beg the sister.

The sister was surprised at what was happening. She did not understand why the man had to slap her on the chest when he was the one who invited her to preach to him. Meanwhile she could notice that life was going out of the man as he continued to beg her to rescue him. So, she prayed for him and he recovered. He asked the sister, "What kind of power do you have?" He told her that for the past 21 years, he had sacrificed a virgin every year to his idol. He would simply call them into his house, slap them and they would fall down and he would cut off any part of their body that he needed for his rituals.

The man could recognize a virgin if he saw one, but when he tried this sister, he met with failure. Why? It was because the sister knew her God and was obedient to Him. Unfortunately, many sisters are ashamed of preaching the gospel. Some men too, are ashamed of sharing the gospel. They fail to realise that the more you witness, the more power flows into your life.

Be vigilant for the devil, your adversary, walketh about seeking whom he may devour. If you notice that the time you spend in praying is reducing, or that your Bible reading no longer makes sense, or you find that fasting is becoming problematic and that going to church is not enjoyable to you anymore, you better shake yourself loose and start praying because the devil, your adversary, walketh about seeking whom he may devour.

The reason he is seeking whom he may devour is because he cannot devour everybody. There are some people he cannot touch. The Bible says, "Christians, seek not yet repose, hear your guardian angel say, thou art in the midst of foes, watch and pray."

A certain sister employed a nanny. Anytime the nanny was bathing the child, the child would be screaming his head out, and after the bath too, he would continue to cry for almost an hour. One day, the sister prayed and the Lord opened her eyes and she found that the nanny was pouring pepper spiritually into the water that she was using in bathing the child. Then she understood. If you want to employ a houseboy, be vigilant. If you want to drink tea and you don't know where it comes from, be vigilant. If you want to put something in your mouth, be vigilant. If you want to go to this party or that party, be vigilant. It is not compulsory for you to honour every invitation. Some of them may be traps. Beloved, you must be sober and vigilant.

PRAYER POINTS:

1. I will not abort the programme of God for my life, in Jesus' name.

2. Oh Lord, set my inner clock for divine appointment, in the name of Jesus.

3. Every power suppressing my elevation, fall down and die, in Jesus' name.

4. Every demonic panel set up against me, scatter unto desolation, in Jesus' name.

5. Every satanic padlock in my hometown working against me, I command you to be roasted, in Jesus' name.

OTHER BOOKS BY DR. D. K. OLUKOYA

1. 20 Marching Orders To Fulfill Your Destiny
2. A-Z of Complete Deliverance
3. Abraham's Children in Bondage
4. Be Prepared
5. Bewitchment must die
6. Biblical Principles of Dream Interpretation
7. Born Great, But Tied Down
8. Breaking Bad Habits
9. Breakthrough Prayers For Business Professionals
10. Brokenness
11. Bringing Down The Power of God
12. Can God?
13. Can God Trust You?
14. Command The Morning
15. Consecration Commitment & Loyalty
16. Contending For The Kingdom
17. Connecting to The God of Breakthroughs
18. Criminals In The House Of God
19. Dancers At The Gate of Death
20. Dealing With Hidden Curses
21. Dealing With Local Satanic Technology
22. Dealing With Satanic Exchange
23. Dealing With The Evil Powers Of Your Father's House
24. Dealing With Tropical Demons
25. Dealing With Unprofitable Roots
26. Dealing With Witchcraft Barbers
27. Deliverance By Fire
28. Deliverance From Spirit Husband And Spirit Wife
29. Deliverance From The Limiting Powers
30. Deliverance of The Brain
31. Deliverance Of The Conscience
32. Deliverance Of The Head
33. Deliverance: God's Medicine Bottle

34. Destiny Clinic
35. Destroying Satanic Masks
36. Disgracing Soul Hunters
37. Divine Military Training
38. Divine Yellow Card
39. Dominion Prosperity
40. Drawers Of Power From The Heavenlies
41. Evil Appetite
42. Evil Umbrella
43. Facing Both Ways
44. Failure In The School Of Prayer
45. Fire For Life's Journey
46. For We Wrestle ...
47. Freedom Indeed
48. Holiness Unto The Lord
49. Holy Cry
50. Holy Fever
51. Hour Of Decision
52. How To Obtain Personal Deliverance
53. How To Pray When Surrounded By The Enemies
54. Idols Of The Heart
55. Is This What They Died For?
56. Let God Answer By Fire
57. Lord, Behold Their Threatening
58. Limiting God
59. Madness Of The Heart
60. Making Your Way Through The Traffic Jam of Life
61. Meat For Champions
62. Medicine For Winners
63. My Burden For The Church
64. Open Heavens Through Holy Disturbance
65. Overpowering Witchcraft
66. Paralysing The Riders And The Horse
67. Personal Spiritual Check-Up

68. Possessing The Tongue of Fire
69. Power Against Coffin Spirits
70. Power Against Destiny Quenchers
71. Power Against Dream Criminals
72. Power Against Local Wickedness
73. Power Against Marine Spirits
74. Power Against Spiritual Terrorists
75. Power To Recover Your Lost Glory
76. Power Must Change Hands
77. Pray Your Way To Breakthroughs
78. Prayer Is The Battle
79. Prayer Rain
80. Prayer Strategies For Spinsters And Bachelors
81. Prayer To Kill Enchantment
82. Prayer To Make You Fulfill Your Divine Destiny
83. Prayer Warfare Against 70 Mad Spirits
84. Prayers For Open Heavens
85. Prayers To Destroy Diseases And Infirmities
86. Prayers To Move From Minimum To Maximum
87. Praying Against The Spirit Of The Valley
88. Praying To Destroy Satanic Roadblocks
89. Praying To Dismantle Witchcraft
90. Principles Of Prayer
91. Release From Destructive Covenants
92. Revoking Evil Decrees
93. Safeguarding Your Home
94. Satanic Diversion Of The Black Race
95. Seventy Sermons To Preach To Your Destiny
96. Silencing The Birds Of Darkness
97. Slaves Who Love Their Chains
98. Smite The Enemy And He Will Flee
99. Speaking Destruction Unto The Dark Rivers
100. Spiritual Education
101. Spiritual Growth And Maturity

102.	Spiritual Warfare And The Home
103.	Strategic Praying
104.	Strategy Of Warfare Praying
105.	Stop Them Before They Stop You
106.	Students In The School Of Fear
107.	Symptoms Of Witchcraft Attack
108.	The Baptism of Fire
109.	The Battle Against The Spirit Of Impossibility
110.	The Dinning Table Of Darkness
111.	The Enemy Has Done This
112.	The Evil Cry Of Your Family Idol
113.	The Fire Of Revival
114.	The Great Deliverance
115.	The Internal Stumbling Block
116.	The Lord Is A Man Of War
117.	The Mystery Of Mobile Curses
118.	The Mystery Of The Mobile Temple
119.	The Prayer Eagle
120.	The Power of Aggressive Prayer Warriors
121.	The Pursuit Of Success
122.	The Seasons Of Life
123.	The Secrets Of Greatness
124.	The Serpentine Enemies
125.	The Skeleton In Your Grandfather's Cupboard
126.	The Slow Learners
127.	The Snake In The Power House
128.	The Spirit Of The Crab
129.	The star hunters
130.	The Star In Your Sky
131.	The Terrible Agenda
132.	The Tongue Trap
133.	The Unconquerable Power
134.	The Unlimited God
135.	The Vagabond Spirit

136.	The Way Of Divine Encounter
137.	The Wealth Transfer Agenda
138.	Tied Down In The Spirits
139.	Too Hot To Handle
140.	Turnaround Breakthrough
141.	Unprofitable Foundations
142.	Vacancy For Mad Prophets
143.	Victory Over Satanic Dreams
144.	Victory Over Your Greatest Enemies
145.	Violent Prayers Against Stubborn Situations
146.	War At The Edge Of Breakthroughs
147.	Wasting The Wasters
148.	Wealth Must Change Hands
149.	What You Must Know About The House Fellowship
150.	When God Is Silent
151.	When the Battle is from Home
152.	When The Deliverer Need Deliverance
153.	When Things Get Hard
154.	When You Are Knocked Down
155.	Where Is Your Faith
156.	While Men Slept
157.	Woman! Thou Art Loosed.
158.	Your Battle And Your Strategy
159.	Your Foundation And Destiny
160.	Your Mouth And Your Deliverance

YORUBA PUBLICATIONS

1. ADURA AGBAYORI
2. ADURA TI NSI OKE NIDI
3. OJO ADURA

FRENCH PUBLICATIONS

1. PLUIE DE PRIERE
2. ESPIRIT DE VAGABONDAGE
3. EN FINIR AVEC LES FORCES MALEFIQUES DE LA MAISON DE TON PERE
4. QUE I'ENVOUTEMENT PERISSE
5. FRAPPEZ I'ADVERSAIRE ET IL FUIRA
6. COMMENT RECEVIOR LA DELIVRANCE DU MARI ET FEMME DE NUIT
7. CPMMENT SE DELIVRER SOI-MEME
8. POVOIR CONTRE LES TERRORITES SPIRITUEL
9. PRIERE DE PERCEES POUR LES HOMMES D'AFFAIRES
10. PRIER JUSQU'A REMPORTER LA VICTOIRE
11. PRIERES VIOLENTES POUR HUMILIER LES PROBLEMES OPINIATRES
12. PRIERE POUR DETRUIRE LES MALADIES ET INFIRMITES
13. LE COMBAT SPIRITUEL ET LE FOYER
14. BILAN SPIRITUEL PERSONNEL
15. VICTOIRES SUR LES REVES SATANIQUES
16. PRIERES DE COMAT CONTRE 70 ESPIRITS DECHANINES
17. LA DEVIATION SATANIQUE DE LA RACE NOIRE
18. TON COMBAT ET TA STRATEGIE
19. VOTRE FONDEMENT ET VOTRE DESTIN

20. REVOQUER LES DECRETS MALEFIQUES
21. CANTIQUE DES CONTIQUES
22. LE MAUVAIS CRI DES IDOLES
23. QUAND LES CHOSES DEVIENNENT DIFFICILES
24. LES STRATEGIES DE PRIERES POUR LES CELIBATAIRES
25. SE LIBERER DES ALLIANCES MALEFIQUES
26. DEMANTELER LA SORCELLERIE
27. LA DELIVERANCE: LE FLACON DE MEDICAMENT DIEU
28. LA DELIVERANCE DE LA TETE
29. COMMANDER LE MATIN
30. NE GRAND MAIS LIE
31. POUVOIR CONTRE LES DEMOND TROPICAUX
32. LE PROGRAMME DE TRANFERT DE RICHESSE
33. LES ETUDIANTS A l'ECOLE DE LA PEUR
34. L'ETOILE DANS VOTRE CIEL
35. LES SAISONS DE LA VIE
36. FEMME TU ES LIBEREE

About the book

Abraham's Children in Trouble introduces a hidden mystery. It highlights the reason behind the high spate of satanic attacks in recent times.

The author has handle the mystery of suffering and attacks in a masterly manner.

The high point of the book is the unfolding of the antidotes to satanic attacks. The are powerful principle on how to tackle the enemy and enjoy the benefit of sonship.

This book we make your life untouchable. The explosive revelations which dot the page of the explosive book will flag off a new beginning in your life.

About the Author

Dr. D. K. Olukoya is the general overseer of the Mountain of Fire and Miracles Ministries and The Battle Cry Christian Ministries.

The Mountain of Fire Miracles Ministries' Headquarters is the largest single Christian congregation in Africa with attendance of over 120,000 in single meetings.

MFM is a full gospel ministry devoted to the revival of Apostolic signs, Holy Ghost Fireworks, miracles and the unlimited demonstration of the power of God to deliver to the uttermost. Absolute holiness within and without as spiritual insecticide and pre-requisite for heaven is openly taught. MFM is a do –it-yourself Gospel Ministry, where your hands are trained to wage war and your fingers to do battle.

Dr. Olukoya hold a first class honours degree in Microbiology from the University of Lagos and PhD in Molecular Genetic from the University of Reading. United Kingdom. As a researcher, he has over seventy scientific publications to his credit.

Anointed by God, Dr. Olukoya is a prophet, evangelist, teacher and preacher of the Word. His Life and that of his wife, Shade and their son Elijah Toluwani are living proofs that all power belong to God.

www.ingramcontent.com/pod-product-compliance
Lightning Source LLC
LaVergne TN
LVHW051204080426
835508LV00021B/2799